Published By Nicholas Thompson

@ Lewis Eaton

Pegan Diet and Cooking Tips for Beginners

ISBN 978-87-94477-48-2

TABLE OF CONTENTS

Ginger And Chicken Brown Rice Pasta

Ingredients:

- ½ medium sweet red pepper, chopped

- ½ cup carrots, grated

- ½ cup red cabbage, chopped

- ¼ tsp ground pepper

- 1 tbsp coconut oil

- 2 tsp garlic, paste

- ¼ tsp ground ancho chile pepper, or chili of choice

- 2 cups uncooked black rice pasta or noodles

- 1 rotisserie chicken, shredded and skin removed

- 2 green onions, chopped

- ½ small red onion, sliced

- 1 ½ cups fresh Brussels sprouts, chopped

- 2 tsp ginger, paste

- ½ tsp salt (optional)

Directions:

1. Cook the pasta as directed.
2. While it is cooking, heat the coconut oil in a large skillet.
3. Add the ginger and garlic paste with the red onion and sauté for 3 minutes.
4. Add the vegetables with the salt, pepper, and ground chili of choice. Cook until all the vegetables are tender with some crunch. This should take about 4–6 minutes.
5. Add the shredded chicken and cook the mixture through.
6. When draining the pasta, retain a cup of the pasta water.

7. Add the pasta and vegetable mixture.

8. Mix to coat all the pasta; if a little dry, add some of the pasta water that was saved.

9. Serve with a sprinkle of green onions.

Mushroom Cauliflower Rice

Ingredients:

- 3 cups mushrooms, sliced

- 1 garlic clove, minced

- ½ cup onion, chopped

- ⅓ cup vegetable broth

- 1 tbsp fresh parsley, chopped

- 1 stick celery, sliced

- 2 cups spinach

- 2 tbsp olive oil

- 14 oz cauliflower florets

- Soy sauce to taste

- Salt and black pepper to taste

Directions:

1. To create cauliflower rice, add the florets to a food processor and pulse it for about 25–30 seconds until it has a rice-like consistency. Set this aside for later use.
2. Add olive oil to a large skillet and heat to medium heat.
3. Add the celery and onion and cook for about five minutes until the vegetables are tender.
4. Add the garlic and cook for a further 30 seconds.
5. Include the mushrooms and sauté until fully cooked through.
6. Now include the cauliflower rice, soy sauce, and vegetable broth.
7. Cook until the cauliflower rice is soft and has absorbed the vegetable broth. Do not allow it to become soggy.
8. Add the spinach and cook lightly for another 3 minutes.

9. Season with salt and pepper and garnish
    before serving.

Lemon-Raspberry Buckwheat Muffins

Ingredients:

For streusel topping:

- ¼ cup (23 g) sliced almonds

- 2 tablespoons (15 g) buckwheat flour

- 2 tablespoons (20 g) coconut sugar

- 2 tablespoons (28 g) pastured butter, melted

For muffins

- 1 teaspoon sea salt

- 2 small ripe bananas

- 4 large pastured eggs

- ½ cup (1 stick; 112 g) pastured butter, melted

- 2 teaspoons vanilla extract

- 1 cup (120 g) raw buckwheat groats

- 1 cup (96 g) almond flour

- 6 tablespoons (54 g) coconut sugar

- 2 teaspoons baking powder

- 3 tablespoons (18 g) grated lemon zest

- 3 tablespoons (45 ml) fresh lemon juice

- 1½ cups (190 g) organic raspberries, fresh or frozen

Directions:

1. To make the streusel topping: In a small bowl, stir together the streusel topping ingredients. Set aside.

2. To make the muffins: In a blender, process the buckwheat grouts until a light, fine flour forms.

3. Measure and reserve 1 cup (100 g) of buckwheat flour for this recipe and store any remaining flour in an airtight container for future use.

4. Preheat the oven to 350°F (180°C, or gas mark 4). Prepare a standard muffin tin by lining it with parchment paper liners. Using parchment liners rather than standard cupcake papers ensures the muffins slip out easily. Set aside.

5. In a large bowl, whisk the reserved buckwheat flour, almond flour, coconut sugar, baking powder, and salt to mix the dry Ingredients: fully.

6. In a medium-size bowl, mash the bananas with a fork into a purée. Add the eggs, melted butter, vanilla, lemon zest, and lemon juice. Mix well. Pour the wet Ingredients: into the dry ingredients, and stir to combine, using fewer than 10 strokes.

7. Fold the raspberries into the batter. Evenly divide the batter among the 12 liners. Top each muffin with 1 heaping teaspoon of streusel topping.

8. Bake for 25 to 28 minutes until the centers are set.

9. Let cool completely. Refrigerate leftovers in an airtight container for up to 7 days, or freeze for up to 3 months.

Sausage, Zucchini, And Apple Fritters

Ingredients:

- ½ teaspoon sea salt

- Black pepper to taste

- 12 ounces (340 g) organic maple breakfast sausage

- 1 large pastured egg

- 4 cups (480 g) grated zucchini

- 1½ cups (225 g) diced apple (I like Pink Lady or H2ycrisp)

- 1 tablespoon (3 g) chopped fresh sage

- 3 tablespoons (45 ml) avocado oil

Directions:

1. In a large bowl, combine the zucchini, apple, sage, salt, and pepper to taste. Use a fork to mix the Ingredients: well.

2. Add the sausage and egg and mix with a fork to combine with the other ingredients.

3. The sausage might be sticky and difficult to incorporate, but continue gently pressing and spreading it into the zucchini mixture.

4. Heat a skillet over medium-low heat and drizzle in the avocado oil.

5. Working in batches, scoop ¼ cup (about 80 g) of the mixture, compact it into a patty, and add it to the hot skillet. Use a spatula to flatten each mound slightly. Cover the skillet and cook for about 10 minutes.

6. Flip each fritter, leaving skillet uncovered, and cook for 6 to 8 minutes more to brown the other side. Repeat with the remaining zucchini mixture until all the fritters are cooked. Serve hot.

7. Cool any leftovers and refrigerate them in an
   airtight container for up to 3 days.

Bbq Chicken Pizza

Ingredients:

- 1 cup mozzarella OR Italian blend shredded cheese

- 1 small onion sliced

- ¼ teaspoon Italian seasoning

- 1 cup chicken breasts, shredded

- ¼ cup fav healthy BBQ sauce

- 1 paleo pizza crust* see recipe below

Directions:

1. Preheat oven to 350.
2. Make paleo pizza crust and spread on BBQ sauce.
3. Top with shredded chicken, cheese, onion, seasoning.

4.   Cook 12-14 minutes.

Pizza Crust

Ingredients:

- 1/3 teaspoon sea salt

- ½ cup olive oil

- ½ cup warm water

- ¾ cup + 2 tablespoons tapioca flour

- 1/3 cup + 2 tablespoons coconut flour

- 1 large egg

Directions:

1. Preheat oven to 450 and prepare pizza st2.

2. Mix together tapioca flour, coconut flour, and salt. Pour in olive oil and water. Add in egg and stir well.

3. Dough should be a little sticky, form into a ball and empty unto a hard surface sprinkled with

tapioca flour. Knead 1-3 minutes or until it forms a non-sticky ball.

4. Transfer unto parchment parch and with a rolling pin dusted with tapioca powder roll out dough to a 12-14-inch crust. If needed dust rolling pin or pizza with more tapioca flour. However, stay mindful of how much is used as to much will make it dense.

5. Transfer rolled out dough to prepared pizza st2 and bake 12-15 minutes.

Friendly Meatless Taco Meat

Ingredients:

Taco meat

- ½ cup sliced baby shitake or button mushrooms

- 2 teaspoons olive oil or avocado oil

- 2 tablespoons nutritional yeast

- ¾ cup +1 tablespoon chopped walnuts

- 1 cup cauliflower florets

Taco spice mixture

- 1 teaspoon oregano

- ¼ teaspoon pepper

- 1 tablespoon coconut sugar

- ½ tablespoon organic h2y

- 1 ½ teaspoons chili powder

- 1 ½ teaspoons of smoked paprika

- ½ teaspoon garlic powder

- 1 teaspoon cumin

- ½ teaspoons onion powder

Directions:

1. Preheat 350

2. Toast walnuts by spreading on baking tray and cooking about 10 minutes.

3. Turn oven up to 400

4. Transfer to a bowl then place cauliflower, sliced mushrooms to the sheet. Drizzle with oil and roast 18-22 minutes or until edges of cauliflower starts to turn at edges.

5. Meanwhile mix together chili powder, smoked paprika, garlic powder, cumin, onion powder, pepper, oregano, coconut sugar, organic h2y.

6. Blend together walnuts, nutritional yeast, and spice mix together and 1 teaspoon at a time mix into meat. Once desired taste is achieved store remaining mix in an airtight container in the refrigerator.

7. Make ahead will keep 5 days in fridge or 1 month in freezer!

Asparagus And Walnut Sauté

Ingredients:

- ¾ pound asparagus, trimmed

- ¼ cup walnuts, chopped

- 1 and ½ tablespoons olive oil

- Salt and pepper to taste

Directions:

1. Place a skillet over medium heat, add olive oil and let it heat up
2. Add asparagus, Sauté for 5 minutes until browned
3. Season with salt and pepper
4. Remove heat
5. Add walnuts and toss
6. Serve warm!

Blackberry Chicken Wings

Ingredients:

- ½ cup blackberry chipotle jam

- Salt and pepper to taste

- 3 pounds chicken wings, about 20 pieces

- ½ cup of water

Directions:

1. Add water and jam to a bowl and mix well
2. Place chicken wings in a zip bag and add 3-thirds of the marinade
3. Season with salt and pepper
4. Let it marinate for 30 minutes
5. Preheat your oven to 400 degrees F
6. Prepare a baking sheet and wire rack, place chicken wings in the wire rack and bake for 15 minutes

7. Brush remaining marinade and bake for 30 minutes more

8. Enjoy!

Apple, Banana, And Berry Smoothie

Ingredients:

- 2 bananas, peeled

- 1 large apple, peeled, cored, diced

- 2 cups almond milk, unsweetened

- 2 cups frozen strawberries

- 2 tablespoons peanut butter

Directions:

1. In the container of a high-speed food processor or blender, combine all of the Ingredients: in the order specified in the Ingredients: list and then cover with the lid.

2. Pulse for 1 minute until smooth, and then serve.

Berry Ginger Zing Smoothie

Ingredients:

- 1 cup frozen raspberries

- 1 cup of frozen strawberries

- 1 cup cauliflower florets

- 2 cups almond milk, unsweetened

- 1-inch pieces of ginger

Directions:

1. In the container of a high-speed food processor or blender, combine all of the Ingredients: in the order specified in the Ingredients: list and then cover with the lid.

2. Pulse for 1 minute until smooth, and then serve.

Garden Egg Salad

Ingredients:

- Kosher salt and freshly ground black pepper

- 2 scallions (white and green), thinly sliced,

- 1 rib celery, minced, scant 1/2 cup

- 2 radishes, grated on the large holes of a box grater

- 8 romaine lettuce leaves

- 6 large eggs

- 1/2 cup low-fat mayonnaise

- 2 tablespoons whole-grain mustard

- 1 cup pea or other sprouts

Directions:

1. Put the eggs in a saucepan with enough cold
    water to cover. Bring to a boil, cover, and
    remove from the heat. Set aside for 12
    minutes.
2. Drain the eggs and roll them between your
    palm and the counter to crack the shell, then
    peel under cool running water.
3. Dice the eggs. Combine the eggs with
    mayonnaise, mustard and season with the salt
    and pepper. Stir in the scallions, celery, and
    radish.
4. Divide the egg salad among the lettuce leaves,
    top with the sprouts and roll up. Serve 2 rolls
    per serving.

Almond Flour Banana Bread

Ingredients:

- Pinch of salt

- 3 ripe bananas, mashed

- 3 eggs

- ¼ cup maple syrup

- ¼ cup melted coconut oil

- 1 teaspoon vanilla extract

- 2 cups almond flour

- ½ teaspoon baking soda

- ½ teaspoon ground cinnamon

- Optional add-ins: chopped nuts, dark chocolate chips, or dried fruits

Directions:

1. Preheat the oven to 350°F (175°C). Set aside a loaf pan that has been greased.
2. In a large bowl, whisk together almond flour, baking soda, ground cinnamon, and salt.
3. In a separate bowl, combine mashed bananas, eggs, maple syrup, melted coconut oil, and vanilla extract. Mix well.
4. Pour the wet Ingredients: into the dry Ingredients: and stir until just combined.
5. If desired, fold in your choice of optional add-ins.
6. Smooth the top of the batter in the greased loaf pan.
7. 45-55 minutes, or until a toothpick inserted into the center comes out clean.
8. Remove from the oven and cool for 10 minutes in the pan before transferring to a wire rack to finish cooling.

9. Slice and enjoy this moist and flavorful almond flour banana bread.

Vegan Chocolate Chip Cookies

Ingredients:

- ¼ teaspoon salt

- ¼ cup coconut oil, melted

- ¼ cup maple syrup

- 2 tablespoons almond butter

- 1 teaspoon vanilla extract

- 1 ½ cups almond flour

- ½ cup coconut flour

- ½ teaspoon baking soda

- ½ cup dairy-free dark chocolate chips

Directions:

1. Preheat the oven to 350°F (175°C). Line a baking sheet with parchment paper and set aside.
2. In a large bowl, whisk together almond flour, coconut flour, baking soda, and salt.
3. In a separate bowl, combine melted coconut oil, maple syrup, almond butter, and vanilla extract. Mix well.
4. Stir the wet Ingredients: into the dry Ingredients: until they are just combined.
5. Fold in the dark chocolate chips.
6. Roll tablespoon-sized portions of the dough into balls and place them on the prepared baking sheet. Flatten each ball slightly with your palm or the back of a spoon.
7. Bake for 12-15 minutes, or until the edges are golden brown.
8. Remove from the oven and let the cookies cool on the baking sheet for 5 minutes before

transferring them to a wire rack to cool

completely.

9. Enjoy these vegan chocolate chip cookies as a
delightful treat.

Baked Garlic Herb Tofu

Ingredients:

- 4 cloves of garlic, minced

- 2 tablespoon of dried mixed herbs (such as thyme, rosemary, and oregano)

- 1/2 teaspoon salt

- 1/4 teaspoon black pepper

- 2 block of firm tofu drained and pressed

- 4 tablespoons soy sauce

- 3 tablespoons of olive oil

- Fresh parsley, chopped (for garnish)

Directions:

1. Preheat the oven to 400°F (200°C) and line a baking sheet with parchment paper.

2. Cut the tofu into 1/2-inch thick slices and pat them dry with a paper towel.

3. In a small bowl, whisk together the soy sauce, olive oil, minced garlic, dried herbs, salt, and black pepper.

4. Place the tofu slices in a shallow dish and pour the marinade over them. Gently toss the tofu to coat each slice evenly.

5. Let the tofu marinate for about 10 minutes, flipping the slices halfway through to ensure even absorption of flavours.

6. Arrange the marinated tofu slices on the prepared baking sheet, leaving space between each slice.

7. Bake in the preheated oven for 20-25 minutes or until the tofu turns golden brown and slightly crispy on the edges.

8. Remove the baked tofu from the oven and allow it to cool for a few minutes.

9. Garnish with freshly chopped parsley before
    serving.

10. Serve the baked garlic herb tofu as a main
    dish or use it as a protein-rich addition to
    salads, stir-fries, or sandwiches.

Stuffed Acorn Squash With Quinoa And Cranberries

Ingredients:

- 2 small onion, finely chopped

- 3 cloves garlic, minced

- 2 teaspoon of dried thyme

- 1/2 teaspoon ground cinnamon

- 1/2 cup dried cranberries

- 1/2 cup chopped pecans

- 2 acorn squashes

- 1 cup quinoa, rinsed

- 2 cups vegetable broth

- 2 tablespoon of olive oil

- Salt and pepper to taste

Directions:

1. Preheat your oven to 375°F (190°C). Cut the acorn squashes in half lengthwise and scoop out the seeds and membranes.

2. Place them cut side down on a baking sheet lined with parchment paper. Bake for about 30-35 minutes or until the flesh is tender.

3. While the squashes are baking, prepare the quinoa. In a medium saucepan, bring the vegetable broth to a boil.

4. Add the rinsed quinoa, reduce the heat to low, cover, and simmer for 15-20 minutes or until all the liquid is absorbed and the quinoa is tender. Set aside.

5. heat the olive oil over medium heat in a large skillet. Add the chopped onion and minced garlic, and sauté until the onion is translucent and fragrant about 5 minutes.

6. Stir in the dried thyme and ground cinnamon, and cook for another minute.

7. Remove the skillet from the heat and add the cooked quinoa, dried cranberries, and chopped pecans. Mix well to combine all the ingredients. Season with salt and pepper to taste.

8. Once the acorn squashes are d2 baking, remove them from the oven and carefully flip them over so the cut side faces up.

9. Divide the quinoa stuffing evenly among the squash halves, pressing it down gently.

10. Return the stuffed squashes to the oven and bake for another 20-25 minutes or until the tops are golden brown and the squashes are completely tender.

11. Remove from the oven and let the stuffed squashes cool for a few minutes before serving. Enjoy!

Grilled Eggplant Salad

Ingredients:

- 2 yellow bell pepper, diced

- 2 small red onion, thinly sliced

- 1 cup cherry tomatoes, halved

- 1/4 cup Kalamata olives, pitted and halved

- 1/4 cup fresh parsley, chopped

- 1/4 cup fresh mint leaves, chopped

- 1/4 cup crumbled feta cheese

- 3 medium-sized eggplants

- 3 tablespoons extra-virgin olive oil

- 3 cloves garlic, minced

- 2 red bell pepper, diced

- Juice of 1 lemon

- Salt and pepper to taste

Directions:

1. Preheat the grill to medium-high heat.

2. Slice the eggplants into 1/2-inch thick rounds. Brush both sides of the eggplant slices with olive oil and season with salt and pepper.

3. Grill the eggplant slices for about 3-4 minutes on each side until they are tender and have nice grill marks. Remove from the grill and let them cool slightly.

4. Once cooled, cut the grilled eggplant slices into bite-sized pieces.

5. In a large bowl, combine the minced garlic, diced bell peppers, sliced red onion, cherry tomatoes, Klamath olives, parsley, and mint leaves.

6. Add the grilled eggplant pieces to the bowl and gently toss to combine all the ingredients.

7. Drizzle the lemon juice over the salad and season with additional salt and pepper to taste. Toss again to coat everything evenly.

8. Sprinkle the crumbled feta cheese over the top of the salad.

9. Serve the Mediterranean Grilled Eggplant Salad immediately or refrigerate for a couple of hours to allow the flavors to meld together.

Zucchini Fritters With Cashew Sour Cream

Ingredients:

For the fritters

- 1/4 cup chickpea flour (or other gluten-free flour)

- 2 tablespoons nutritional yeast

- 1 teaspoon garlic powder

- 1/2 teaspoon dried dill

- 2 medium zucchinis, grated

- 1/2 small onion, grated

- Salt and pepper to taste

- Coconut oil for frying

For the cashew sour cream

- Juice of 1 lemon

- 1 tablespoon apple cider vinegar

- 1/4 cup water

- 1 cup raw cashews, soaked in water for 2 hours

- Salt to taste

Directions:

For the fritters

1. Place the grated zucchinis in a colander and sprinkle them with a pinch of salt. Let them sit for 10-15 minutes to release excess moisture.
2. Squeeze the grated zucchinis to remove the excess liquid.
3. In a large bowl, combine the grated zucchinis, grated onion, chickpea flour, nutritional yeast, garlic powder, dried dill, salt, and pepper. Mix well to form a batter.
4. Heat a non-stick skillet over medium heat and add a small amount of coconut oil.
5. Drop spoonful of the zucchini batter onto the skillet, flattening them slightly with a spatula.
6. Cook the fritters for 3-4 minutes on each side, or until golden brown and crispy.
7. Remove the fritters from the skillet and place them on a paper towel-lined plate to absorb any excess oil.

For the cashew sour cream

8. Drain and rinse the soaked cashews.

9. In a blender or food processor, combine the cashews, lemon juice, apple cider vinegar, water, and salt. Blend until smooth and creamy.

10. Taste and adjust the seasoning if needed.

11. Serve the zucchini fritters warm with a dollop of cashew sour cream on top.

Roasted Chickpeas With Spices

Ingredients:

- 1 teaspoon smoked paprika

- 1/2 teaspoon ground cumin

- 1/2 teaspoon garlic powder

- 1/4 teaspoon cayenne pepper (optional for spice)

- 1 can chickpeas, drained and rinsed

- 1 tablespoon olive oil

- Salt to taste

Directions:

1. Preheat the oven to 400°F (200°C) and line a baking sheet with parchment paper.
2. Pat the chickpeas dry with a clean kitchen towel or paper towel.

3. In a bowl, toss the chickpeas with olive oil, smoked paprika, ground cumin, garlic powder, cayenne pepper (if using), and salt until evenly coated.

4. Spread the seas2d chickpeas in a single layer on the prepared baking sheet.

5. Roast the chickpeas in the preheated oven for 25-30 minutes, shaking the pan halfway through, until they are crispy and golden brown.

6. Remove from the oven and let them cool slightly before serving.

7. Enjoy the roasted chickpeas as a crunchy and protein-packed snack.

Guacamole With Veggie Sticks

Ingredients:

- 1/4 cup finely chopped red onion

- 2 tablespoons freshly squeezed lime juice

- 2 tablespoons chopped fresh cilantro

- 2 ripe avocados

- 1 small tomato, diced

- Salt and pepper to taste

- Assorted veggie sticks for dipping (e.g., carrot sticks, cucumber slices, bell pepper strips)

Directions:

1. Cut the avocados in half, remove the pits, and scoop the flesh into a bowl.

2. Mash the avocado with a fork until desired consistency.

3. Add the diced tomato, chopped red onion,
   lime juice, chopped cilantro, salt, and pepper
   to the bowl.

4. Mix well to combine.

5. Taste and adjust the seasoning if needed.

6. Serve the guacamole with veggie sticks for a
   refreshing and nutritious snack or appetizer.

Sweet Potato & Bell Pepper Hash

Ingredients:

- 1 seeded and chopped small red bell pepper

- 1 tbsp. olive oil

- 1 seeded and chopped small green bell pepper

- Salt

- 1 chopped medium onion

- ¼ c. chopped green scallion

- 1 peeled and cubed large sweet potato

- Freshly ground black pepper

- 2 tbsps. water

Directions:

1. Heat oil on a large skillet over medium heat.
    Add onion and sauté for about 2 minutes.

2. Add sweet potato and cook, stirring
    occasionally for about 5 minutes.

3. Add bell peppers and cook for about 1
    minute.

4. Add water and seasonings and stir to
    combine.

5. Cover the skillet and cook, stirring
    occasionally for about 10 minutes.

6. Add scallion and stir then remove from heat
    immediately.

7. Serve hot and enjoy.

Healthy Breakfast Bowl

Ingredients:

- ¼ tsp. ground cinnamon

- 2 c. unsweetened almond milk

- 3 tbsps. sunflower seeds

- 1 peeled and sliced medium banana

- ½ tsp. organic vanilla extract

- 2 peeled, cored and grated large delicious red apples

- 3 tbsps. toasted and chopped almonds

Directions:

1. Mix together grated apples, vanilla extract, almond milk, sunflower seeds, and cinnamon in a large pan on medium-low heat.

2. Gently cook and stir occasionally for about 4
    minutes.

3. Remove from heat and put into serving bowls.

4. Allow to cool slightly.

5. Add a banana slices and almond topping.

6. Serve and enjoy.

Quinoa Salad

Ingredients:

- 1/4 cup cucumbers sliced

- 2 TB red wine vinegar

- 2 TB olive oil good quality

- 1 teaspoon lemon juice fresh-squeezed

- 1/2 teaspoon oregano dried

- 1/2 teaspoon Greek Seasoning Cavender's or any other greek seasoning mix

- 2 cups lettuce greens chopped mixed

- 2 cups quinoa cooked

- 1/2 cup peppers red and yellow, sliced into ribbons

- 1/4 cup onion sweet, chopped

- 1/4 cup olives green and kalamata

- salt to taste

- pepper to taste

Directions:

1. Place all ingredients in a mixing bowl in order given.
2. Toss and serve
3. The addition of chopped broccoli, celery, or green peppers would be delicious.

Salmon-Stuffed Avocados

Ingredients:

- 1 tablespoon lime juice

- 2 teaspoons mayonnaise

- 1 teaspoon Dijon mustard

- ⅛ teaspoon salt

- ⅛ teaspoon ground pepper

- 2 (5 ounce) cans salmon, drained, flaked, skin and b2s removed

- 2 avocados

- ½ cup nonfat plain Greek yogurt

- ½ cup diced celery

- 2 tablespoons chopped fresh parsley

- Chopped chives for garnish

Directions:

1. Combine yogurt, celery, parsley, lime juice, mayonnaise, mustard, salt, and pepper in a medium bowl; mix well. Add salmon and mix well.

2. Halve avocados lengthwise and remove pits. Scoop about 1 tablespoon flesh from each

avocado half into a small bowl. Mash the scooped-out avocado flesh with a fork and stir into the salmon mixture.

3. Fill each avocado half with about 1/4 cup of the salmon mixture, mounding it on top of the avocado halves. Garnish with chives, if desired.

Chocolate Avocado Mousse

Ingredients:

1/four cup maple syrup or another herbal sweetener of your preference

- 1/four cup unsweetened almond milk or coconut milk

- 1 teaspoon vanilla extract

- Pinch of salt

- 2 ripe avocados

- 1/four cup unsweetened cocoa powder

- Optional toppings: shaved darkish chocolate, clean berries, chopped nuts

Directions:

1. Cut the avocados in 1\/2, do away with the pits, and scoop out the flesh right into a blender or meals processor.

2. Add the cocoa powder, maple syrup, almond milk, vanilla extract, and salt to the blender.

3. Blend the comp2nts on excessive velocity till easy and creamy, scraping down the perimeters if necessary.

4. Ensure there aren't any lumps or chunks of avocado final.

5. Taste the mousse and alter the wonder or chocolate depth to your liking by including greater maple syrup or cocoa powder as needed.

6. Transfer the mousse to serving bowls or glasses and refrigerate for a minimum half-hour to permit it to set and corporation up.

7. Before serving, you could garnish the mousse with shaved darkish chocolate, sparkling berries, or chopped nuts for texture and flavor.

8. Enjoy the Chocolate Avocado Mousse chilled, savoring its velvety texture and the harmonious combination of chocolate and avocado flavors.

9. This dessert isn't always the most effective scrumptious however additionally affords an excellent dose of wholesome fat, fiber, and antioxidants from avocados and cocoa powder.

10. The herbal sweetness from maple syrup or different sweeteners makes it a guilt-loose indulgence. Plus, it is vegan, gluten-loose, and

dairy-unfastened, making it appropriate for plenty of nutritional options.

11. Feel free to test with 2-of-a-kind versions in ways including a touch of cinnamon, a touch of almond extract, or a pinch of cayenne pepper for a diffused twist.

12. You also can strive to incorporate different toppings like coconut whipped cream or toasted coconut flakes to beautify the dessert.

13. Chocolate Avocado Mousse is an exceptional manner to revel in a decadent deal at the same time as incorporating nutrient-wealthy comp2nts into your weight-reduction plan.

14. So cross ahead, bask in this creamy delight, and fulfill your cravings with a more fit desire!

Berry Crumble

Ingredients:

For the Filling:

- Four cups blended berries (strawberries, blueberries, raspberries, blackberries)

- 2 tablespoons lemon juice

- 2 tablespoons arrowroot powder or tapioca starch

- 1 tablespoon natural maple syrup or h2y (optional, for delivered sweetness)
  1 teaspoon vanilla extract

For the Crumble Topping:

- 1 cup almond flour

- half of a cup of shredded unsweetened coconut 1/four cup chopped nuts (almonds, walnuts, pecans)

- 2 tablespoons coconut oil, melted

- 2 tablespoons natural maple syrup or h2y 1 teaspoon cinnamon

- Pinch of salt

Directions:

1. Preheat the oven to 350°F (175°C) and gently grease a baking dish.
2. In a huge bowl, integrate the blended berries, lemon juice, arrowroot powder (or tapioca starch), maple syrup (or h2y), and vanilla extract.
3. Toss till the berries are covered lightly.
4. Transfer the berry combination to the greased baking dish and unfold it out in a good layer.

5. In a separate bowl, integrate the almond flour, shredded coconut, chopped nuts, melted coconut oil, maple syrup (or h2y), cinnamon, and salt. Mix till the comp2nts are nicely blended and the aggregate will become crumbly.

6. Sprinkle the disintegrated topping calmly over the berry filling with inside the baking dish.

7. Place the dish within side the preheated oven and bake for 25-half-hour, or till the berries are effervescent and the didisintegratedopping is golden brown.

8. Once baked, get rid of the berry collapse from the oven and permit it to chill for a couple of minutes earlier than serving.

9. Serve the Pegan Berry Crumble heat or at room temperature. You can revel in it on its own or pair it with a dollop of coconut whipped cream or a scoop of dairy-loose vanilla ice cream for delivered indulgence.

10. This Pegan-pleasant Berry Crumble gives a pleasing mixture of candy and tart flavors from the combined berries, whilst the nutty and crunchy collapse topping provides a fulfilling texture.

11. It's a dessert full of antioxidants, wholesome fat, and fiber from berries, nuts, and almond flour.

12. Remember to revel in this dessert in moderation, as even herbal sweeteners can make contributions to normal calorie intake.

13. Feel unfastened to test with unique mixtures of berries or modify the beauty stage to fit your flavor choices.

14. By making easy substitutions and the usage of healthy substances, you may create a scrumptious Berry Crumble that clings to the ideas of a Pegan food plan, permitting you to bask in a satisfying dessert at the same time as staying proper in your nutritional goals.

Tahiti And Kale Salad

Ingredients:

- 2 tablespoons water

- 1 clove garlic, minced

- 1/4 teaspoon salt

- 1/4 teaspoon black pepper

- 1 tablespoon olive oil

- 1 bunch of kale, stems removed and chopped
  into bite-sized pieces

- 1/4 cup tahini

- 2 tablespoons lemon juice

- 1/4 cup chopped almonds

Directions:

1. In a large bowl, combine the chopped kale
    and olive oil. Use your hands to massage the
    oil into the kale for 2-3 minutes, until it
    becomes slightly wilted.

2. In a small bowl, whisk together the tahini,
    lemon juice, water, garlic, salt, and black
    pepper until smooth.

3. Pour the tahini dressing over the kale and toss
    until well coated.

    4. Sprinkle the chopped almonds over the
    salad and serve.

Salmon With Apple And Kale Salad

Ingredients:

- ¼ cup pecorino (sheep's cheese), finely grated

- 3 tbsp lemon juice, fresh

- 3 tbsp olive oil

- 3 tbsp toasted slivered almonds

- 1 apple of choice

- ¼ cup of dates, pitted

- Freshly black pepper, ground

- 6 cups of kale, ribs removed, and leaves sliced very thinly

- 4 salmon fillets, an inch thick and 5 oz each

- 1 tsp salt

- 4 whole wheat dinner rolls (optional)

Directions:

1. Ensure that the salmon is at room temperature 10 minutes before cooking.
2. In a bowl, whisk 2 tablespoons of olive oils, lemon juice, and ¼ teaspoon salt. Then add the kale and coat it thoroughly and allow it to stand for 10 minutes.
3. While waiting, cut the dates into slivers and the apples into thin sticks.
4. Add the apples, cheese, and dates to the kale then season with pepper and toss before setting aside.
5. Using ½ tsp and some pepper, sprinkle both sides of the salmon pieces.
6. In a large skillet, heat a tablespoon of oil to medium-high before placing the salmon in the skillet skin-side up.

7. Cook for about 4 minutes or until the fish is golden brown. Flip the fish and cook for another 3 minutes or until firm to touch.

8. Split the salmon, salad, and rolls between the plates and serve immediately.

Melt Sandwich

Ingredients:

- ½ cup pumpkin seeds, soaked

- 1 cup walnuts, soaked

- ½ cup sunflower seeds, soaked

- ½ lemon, juiced

- ⅓ cup vegan-friendly mayonnaise

- ½ tsp sea salt

- 1 cup grated or 4 slices vegan cheese

- 2 tsp fresh dill, chopped

- 1 cup celery, diced

- 1 cup cucumber, diced

- ¼ cup green onions, chopped

- 2 tsp dulse or kelp flakes

- 8 slices of pegan-friendly bread or sweet
  potato toast

Directions:

1. Soak the pumpkin seeds, sunflower seeds,
    and walnuts for 15 minutes before draining
    and rinsing.
2. Add these to a food processor and blend until
    partially crumbled yet smooth.
3. Place the seed mixture in a bowl then add the
    mayonnaise and stir until fully combined.
4. Add all other ingredients, except for cheese
    and bread, and stir.
5. Place the vegan cheese on the bread then top
    with the mixture from the bowl before adding
    the second piece of bread.
6. You can melt the cheese by adding the
    sandwich to a sandwich maker and cooking
    for between 5–7 minutes to allow the cheese

to melt. This method is best used for vegan bread.

7. Also, you can add the sandwich to a skillet over medium-low heat with a touch of oil to cook four minutes a side until the cheese is melted. This method is better for paleo bread or sweet potato bread.

8. Serve warm with some vegetable sticks.

Endurance Chia Seed Pudding With Berries

Ingredients:

- ¼ teaspoon vanilla extract or almond extract

- Fresh berries, such as blackberries, blueberries, raspberries, or strawberries, for topping (optional)

- Unsweetened shredded coconut, for topping (optional)

- Chopped nuts or seeds, for topping (optional)

- Nut butter, for topping (optional)

- 3 cups (720 ml) unsweetened vanilla Almond Milk (here) or store-bought almond milk

- 2 to 3 tablespoons (40 to 60 g) maple syrup or h2y

- 2 tablespoons (28 g) virgin coconut oil, melted

- ½ cup (96 g) chia seeds

- Chopped 85% dark chocolate, for topping (optional)

Directions:

1. In a blender, combine the almond milk and maple syrup. Blend on low speed. While the blender is running, add the melted coconut oil and process until incorporated.

2. Add the chia seeds and vanilla and pulse to combine. Let sit for 5 to 10 minutes, then pulse 4 or 5 times. Repeat 3 or 4 times until the pudding is thickened.

3. Pour the pudding into storage jars. I like to use small jars, so they are easy to take with me on the go or pull out and top for a quick breakfast or snack.

4. The pudding will continue to thicken as it chills, so it's best to make it several hours

before serving. Top as desired when ready to
serve.

5. The chia seed pudding will keep for 5 to 6
days, refrigerated in airtight jars.

Power-Up Millet Breakfast Bowl

Ingredients:

- 2 cups (298 g) cherry tomatoes

- Sea salt and black pepper to taste

- 1 cup (200 g) millet, cooked according to the package Directions:

- 4 cups (80 g) arugula

- 4 large pastured eggs, cooked to your liking

- 2 tablespoons (30 ml) avocado oil, divided

- 2 cups (140 g) sliced mushrooms

- ¼ cup (38 g) goat cheese crumbles

Directions:

1. In a large skillet over medium heat, heat 1 tablespoon (15 ml) of the avocado oil.

2. Add the mushrooms and tomatoes. Sauté for
    5 to 7 minutes until the tomatoes burst and
    the mushrooms have started to brown. Set
    aside.

3. Drizzle the remaining 1 tablespoon (15 ml) of
    avocado oil into the hot millet, then season it
    with salt and pepper to taste. Evenly divide
    the millet among 4 bowls.

4. Top each bowl with 2-fourth of the sautéed
    mushrooms and tomatoes, 1 cup (20 g) of
    arugula, and 1 egg. Sprinkle each with 1
    tablespoon (about 9 g) of goat cheese.

Veggie Stew

Ingredients:

- 2 zucchinis, sliced

- ¼ cup mushrooms, diced

- 2/3 tablespoon organic tomato paste

- 1 large can petite diced no-salt added tomatoes

- 2 tbs fresh thyme

- 2 cups water, chicken stock, or veggie stock

- ¼ c fresh basil

- 1 tablespoon olive oil or coconut oil

- 1 tsp cayenne powder

- 1/3 cup onion, diced

- 1 clove garlic thinly sliced

- 1/3 cup diced red bell pepper

- 1 large eggplant, cubed

- ¼ c fresh parsley

Directions:

1. In a Dutch oven brought to medium heat add olive oil, cayenne powder, diced onions, garlic slices, diced red bell peppers. Sauté 3-5 minutes.

2. Add in eggplant cubes and zucchini slices let meld 1 minute.

3. Stir in tomato paste, petite diced tomatoes, a liquid. Bring to boil, cover, reduce heat and simmer 20 minutes.

4. Remove from heat and stir in all herbs.

Cauliflower Rice With Baked Sesame Cod

Ingredients:

- 2/3 teaspoon lemon peel

- 1 teaspoon picante seasoning

- 2/3 teaspoon black pepper

- 2 tablespoons pinenuts

- ¼ cup parsley, chopped

- ¼ cup Italian oregano, diced

- 4 filets of cod

- 4 cups cauliflower rice

- 2 teaspoons olive oil

- 1 tablespoon butter or ghee

- 2 tablespoons onion, chopped

- 1 teaspoon garlic, minced

- 3 packet, or 3 cups, chicken stock

Directions:

1. Preheat oven to 350 and prepare 13x13 dish.

2. Place filets in dish and pour liquid around them. Bake 30 minutes.

3. To skillet warmed over medium-high heat add olive oil, butter, onion, garlic sauté 3-5 minutes then stir in cauliflower.

4. Sprinkle over cauliflower picante seasoning, black pepper.

5. Divide amongst four plates and top each with pinenuts, parsley, Italian oregano

6. Servings: 4

Chicken Dinner Casserole

Ingredients:

- 2 cups diced, canned tomatoes, undrained

- 5 garlic cloves, crushed

- 1 teaspoon paprika

- 4 chicken breast halves, skinless and b2less

- 1 pound okra

- 1 big onion, chopped

- Salt and pepper as needed

Directions:

1. Preheat your oven to 350 degrees F
2. Take a large baking dish and place it over medium heat
3. Add oil and let the oil heat up
4. Add onion and Sauté for 2 minutes

5. Add paprika, pepper, garlic, and Sauté for 2 minutes more

6. Stir in okra and tomatoes, remove heat and arrange chicken pieces into the vegies

7. Season with salt and pepper

8. Cover and bake for 40 minutes

9. Gently stir about halfway through

10. Serve and enjoy!

11. for about 10 minutes once d2

12. Enjoy!

Chicken And Basil Zucchini Oodles

Ingredients:

- ¼ cup of coconut milk

- 1 garlic clove, peeled, minced

- 1 zucchini, shredded

- 2 chicken fillets, cubed

- 2 tablespoons ghee

- 1 pound tomatoes, diced

- ½ cup basil, chopped

Directions:

1. Sauté cubed chicken in ghee until no longer pink

2. Add tomatoes and season with salt

3. Simmer and reduce the liquid

4. Prepare your zucchini Zoodles by shredding zucchini in a food processor

5. Add basil, garlic, coconut milk to chicken and cook for a few minutes

6. Add half of the zucchini Zoodles to a bowl and top with creamy tomato basil chicken

7. Enjoy!

Coconut Water Smoothie

Ingredients:

- 1 cup of frozen mango pieces

- 2 teaspoons peanut butter

- 2 cups of coconut water

- 1 large apple, peeled, cored, diced

- 4 teaspoons coconut flakes

Directions:

1. In the container of a high-speed food processor or blender, combine all of the Ingredients: in the order specified in the Ingredients: list and then cover with the lid.
2. Pulse for 1 minute until smooth, and then serve.

Zucchini And Blueberry Smoothie

Ingredients:

- ½ cup spinach leaves, fresh

- 1 cup frozen blueberries

- 2/3 cup sliced zucchini

- 1 tablespoon hemp seeds

- ½ teaspoon maca powder

- 1 cup coconut milk, unsweetened

- 1 large celery stem

- 2 bananas, peeled

- ¼ teaspoon ground cinnamon

Directions:

1. In the container of a high-speed food processor or blender, combine all of the

Ingredients: in the order specified in the Ingredients: list and then cover with the lid.

2. Pulse for 1 minute until smooth, and then serve.

Mixed Berry Chia Seed Pudding

Ingredients:

- 1 tablespoon maple syrup

- 1 teaspoon vanilla extract

- 1 cup berries (strawberries, blueberries, and raspberries)

- ½ cup chia seeds

- 2 cups almond milk (or any plant-based milk)

- Fresh mint leaves for garnish

Directions:

1. In a bowl, combine chia seeds, almond milk, maple syrup, and vanilla extract. Stir well to incorporate the chia seeds.

2. Allow the mixture to sit for 10-15 minutes, stirring every now and then to prevent clumping.

3. After the chia seeds have absorbed the liquid and the mixture has thickened, give it a final stir.

4. Divide the chia seed pudding into serving glasses or bowls.

5. Top with mixed berries and garnish with fresh mint leaves.

6. Refrigerate for at least 2 hours or overnight to allow the pudding to set and flavors to meld.

7. Serve chilled and enjoy the refreshing and nutritious chia seed pudding.

Green Goddess Smoothie

Ingredients:

- ½ cup almond milk (or other plant-based milk)

- 1 tablespoon chia seeds

- 1 tablespoon almond butter

- Optional: 1 teaspoon h2y or maple syrup

- 1 cup spinach

- 1 ripe banana

- ½ avocado

- Ice cubes (optional)

Directions:

1. In a blender, combine spinach, banana, avocado, almond milk, chia seeds, almond butter, and h2y or maple syrup if desired.
2. Blend until smooth and creamy.
3. Add ice cubes if desired, and blend until desired consistency is reached.
4. Pour into a glass and enjoy this refreshing and nutrient-packed green smoothie.

Broccoli And Mushroom Stir-Fry

Ingredients:

- 4 cloves garlic, minced

- 1-inch piece of ginger, grated

- 3 tablespoons of soy sauce

- 2 tablespoon of oyster sauce

- 1 teaspoon sesame oil

- 1/2 teaspoon red pepper flakes (optional)

- 1 large head of broccoli

- 8 ounces mushrooms (such as cremini or button mushrooms), sliced

- 3 tablespoons of vegetable oil

- Salt and pepper to taste

Directions:

1. Cut the broccoli into small florets. Peel the stalk and cut it into thin slices.
2. Heat the vegetable oil in a large skillet or wok over medium-high heat.
3. Add the minced garlic and grated ginger to the skillet and sauté for about 1 minute until fragrant.
4. Add the sliced mushrooms to the skillet and cook for 3-4 minutes until they soften.
5. Add the broccoli florets and sliced stalk to the skillet. Stir-fry for 4-5 minutes until the broccoli is tender-crisp.
6. In a small bowl, whisk together the soy sauce, oyster sauce, sesame oil, and red pepper flakes (if using).
7. Pour the sauce over the vegetables in the skillet and toss to coat evenly. Cook for an additional 1-2 minutes to heat through.
8. Season with salt and pepper to taste.

9. Remove from heat and serve the Broccoli and
    Mushroom Stir-Fry hot as a side dish or over
    steamed rice or noodles.

Baked Falafel With Tahiti Sauce

Ingredients:

For the falafel:

- 2 teaspoon of ground cumin

- 2 teaspoon of ground coriander

- 1/2 teaspoon baking powder

- 3 tablespoons of all-purpose flour

- 2 tablespoon of lemon juice

- Salt and pepper to taste

- 1 ½ cups cooked chickpeas

- 1 small onion, roughly chopped

- 4 cloves garlic, minced

- 1/4 cup fresh parsley, chopped

- 1/4 cup fresh cilantro, chopped

- Olive oil for brushing

For the tahini sauce:

- 3 tablespoons of lemon juice

- 2 tablespoons water

- 2 clove of garlic, minced

- 1/4 cup tahini paste

- Salt to taste

For serving:

- Pita bread or flatbread

- Fresh salad vegetables (lettuce, tomatoes, cucumbers, etc.)

Directions:

1. Preheat your oven to 375°F (190°C).

2. In a food processor, combine the chickpeas,
    onion, garlic, parsley, cilantro, cumin,
    coriander, baking powder, flour, lemon juice,
    salt, and pepper. Pulse the mixture until well
    combined but still slightly chunky. Avoid
    overprocessing.
3. Using your hands, shape the falafel mixture
    into small patties or balls about 1 ½ inches in
    diameter.
4. Place the falafel on a baking sheet lined with
    parchment paper. Brush each falafel with
    olive oil.
5. Bake the falafel in the preheated oven for 20-
    25 minutes or until golden brown and crispy
    on the outside.
6. While the falafel is baking, prepare the tahini
    sauce. In a small bowl, whisk together the
    tahini paste, lemon juice, water, minced
    garlic, and salt until smooth and creamy.

7. Adjust the consistency by adding more water if necessary.

8. Once the falafel is ready, remove it from the oven and let it cool slightly.

9. Serve the baked falafel with pita bread or flatbread, fresh salad vegetables, and a drizzle of tahini sauce. You can also add toppings like sliced tomatoes, cucumbers, or pickles.

Veggie-Packed Omelet

Ingredients:

- 1/4 cup diced zucchini

- 1/4 cup diced tomatoes

- Handful of spinach leaves

- Salt and pepper to taste

- 3 large eggs

- 2 tablespoons unsweetened almond milk

- 1/4 cup diced bell peppers (assorted colors)

- Fresh herbs for garnish (optional)

Directions:

1. In a bowl, whisk together the eggs and almond milk. Season with salt and pepper.

2. Heat a non-stick skillet over medium heat.

3. Add the diced bell peppers and zucchini to the skillet. Sauté for a few minutes until slightly softened.

4. Add the diced tomatoes and spinach leaves to the skillet. Cook for another minute until the spinach wilts.

5. Pour the whisked eggs over the vegetables in the skillet.

6. Cook the omelet for 2-3 minutes, gently lifting the edges and tilting the skillet to allow the uncooked eggs to flow to the edges.

7. Once the omelet is mostly set, carefully flip it over using a spatula or fold it in half.

8. Cook for another minute until the eggs are fully cooked.

9. Slide the omelet onto a plate and garnish with fresh herbs if desired. Serve hot and enjoy!

Chia Pudding With Fresh Fruits

Ingredients:

- 1 cup unsweetened almond milk

- 1 tablespoon maple syrup or h2y

- 1/2 teaspoon vanilla extract

- 3 tablespoons chia seeds

- Fresh fruits for topping (e.g., sliced strawberries, blueberries, sliced banana)

Directions:

1. In a bowl, combine the chia seeds, almond milk, maple syrup (or h2y), and vanilla extract.
2. Stir well to make sure the chia seeds are evenly distributed.
3. Let the mixture sit for about 5 minutes, then stir again to prevent clumping.
4. Cover the bowl and refrigerate overnight or for at least 4 hours, allowing the chia seeds to absorb the liquid and form a pudding-like consistency.

5. When ready to serve, give the chia pudding a good stir.

6. Divide the pudding into individual serving bowls and top with fresh fruits.

7. Enjoy the creamy and nutritious chia pudding!

Coconut Whipped Cream

Ingredients:

- 1-2 tablespoons of sweetener (optional, along with maple syrup or powdered coconut sugar)

- 1 teaspoon of vanilla extract (optional)

- 1 can of full-fat coconut milk or coconut cream (refrigerated in a single day)

Directions:

1. Place the can of coconut milk or coconut cream withinside the fridge for a singledressess s their toll from the liquid.

2. Carefully open the can without shaking it. You will be aware that the cream has solidified on the pinnacle even as the liquid stays on the bottom.

3. Scoop out the solidified coconut cream from the can right into a blending bowl, leaving the

liquid behind (you could store the liquid for different recipes or smoothies).

4. Using a hand mixer or stand mixer, whip the coconut cream at onatedium-excessive velocity till it turns mild and fluffy, equivalent to the feel of whipped cream. This system may also take a couple of minutes.

5. If preferred, upload the sweetener and vanilla extract to the whipped coconut cream. Start with a smaller quantity of sweetener and regulate the flavor. Mix lightly till nicely mixed.

6. Once the coconut whipped cream has reached the preferred consistency and flavor, it is prepared to be served. You can use it straight away or shop it withinside the fridge for later use.

7. Coconut whipped cream is a flexible topping that may be loved in diverse ways. Here are some ideas:

8. Serve it with sparkling berries, sliced fruit, or a
   fruit salad.

9. Top off a slice of Pagan-pleasant pie, tart, or
   disintegrate.

10. Add a dollop for your favored dairy-loose
    warm chocolate or espresso beverage.

11. Use it as a frosting for cakes, cupcakes, or
    different baked goods.

12. Keep in mind that coconut whipped cream
    has a mild coconut flavor, which provides a
    tropical twist for your cakes. If you choose an
    extra impartial flavor, you may upload
    different flavorings along with cocoa powder,
    cinnamon, or citrus zest.

13. Coconut whipped cream is a scrumptious and
    flexible addition to our Pegan dessert
    repertoire.

14. It gives a creamy, dairy-loose choice that is
    enjoyable and appropriate for the 2s following
    a plant-primarily based totally lifestyle.

15. Enjoy the richness and herbal sweetness of
coconut cream on this pleasant whipped
cream opportunity.

Banana Oat Cookies

Ingredients:

- 1 tablespoon coconut oil, melted

- 1 teaspoon vanilla extract

- Optional upload-ins: chopped nuts, seeds, unsweetened shredded coconut, cacao nibs, or cinnamon

- 2 ripe bananas, mashed

- 1 ½ cups rolled oats (gluten-unfastened if necessary)

- ¼ cup nut butter (almond, cashew, or sunflower seed butter)

Directions:

1. Preheat your oven to 350°F (175°C) and line a baking sheet with parchment paper.

2. In a big blending bowl, integrate the mashed bananas, rolled oats, nut butter, melted coconut oil, and vanilla extract.

3. Stir nicely till all of the elements are very well combined.

4. If desired, upload in your selected upload-ins including chopped nuts, seeds, shredded coconut, cacao nibs, or cinnamon. Mix till calmly dispensed during the batter.

5. Take spoonfuls of the aggregate and drop them onto the organized baking sheet, shaping them into cookie-sized rounds. Leave a bit of area among every cookie as they may unfold barely for the duration of baking.

6. Bake with inside the preheated oven for about 15-20 mins or till the cookies are golden brown across the edges.

7. Remove from the oven and allow the cookies to cool on the baking sheet for some mins,

then switch them to a twine rack to chill completely.

8. These banana oat cookies are sweetened with the aid of using bananas and may be loved as a guilt-loose snack.

9. They offer an excellent supply of nutritional fiber from the oats, wholesome fat from the nut butter and coconut oil, and vital nutrients and minerals from any upload-ins you pick to include.

10. Remember, at the same time as those cookies align with the Pegan weight loss plan ideas, it is n2theless crucial to eat them in moderation.

11. Enjoy them as a part of a nicely-rounded and balanced weight loss program that specializes in loads of whole, unprocessed meals.

12. It's well worth noting that nutritional wishes and options can vary, so continually visit a healthcare expert or registered dietitian

earlier than making any substantial adjustments to your weight-reduction plan, such as adopting the Pegan weight loss plan.

Walnut And Sweet Potato Burgers

Ingredients:

- 1/2 tsp smoked paprika

- 1/2 tsp ground cumin

- 1/2 tsp salt

- 1/4 tsp black pepper

- 2 cloves garlic, minced

- 1 large sweet potato, peeled and diced

- 1 cup walnuts

- 1/2 cup breadcrumbs

- 2 tbsp olive oil

Directions:

1. Preheat the oven to 375°F (190°C).

2. Boil the diced sweet potato in a pot of water for about 10 minutes or until tender. Drain and set aside.

3. In a food processor, pulse the walnuts until coarsely chopped.

4. In a large bowl, mix together the chopped walnuts, breadcrumbs, smoked paprika, cumin, salt, black pepper, and minced garlic.

5. Add the boiled sweet potato to the bowl and mix well to combine.

6. Shape the mixture into 6 patties.

7. Heat the olive oil in a large skillet over medium-high heat. Add the patties and cook for 3-4 minutes on each side until browned.

8. Transfer the patties to a baking sheet and bake for 10-15 minutes until heated through.

Roasted Vegetable And Lentil Bowl

Ingredients:

- 2 tablespoons olive oil

- 1 teaspoon smoked paprika

- 1 teaspoon garlic powder

- Salt and black pepper to taste

- 1 cup cooked lentils (either green or brown)

- 1 avocado, sliced

- 1/4 cup crumbled feta cheese (optional)

- 1 medium sweet potato, peeled and chopped into small cubes

- 1 red bell pepper, chopped into small pieces

- 1 yellow bell pepper, chopped into small pieces

- 1 red onion, chopped into small pieces

- Fresh cilantro, chopped (optional)

Directions:

1. Preheat the oven to 425°F (218°C).

2. Place the chopped sweet potato, bell peppers, and red onion on a baking sheet. Drizzle with olive oil and sprinkle with smoked paprika, garlic powder, salt, and black pepper. Toss to coat the vegetables evenly.

3. Roast the vegetables in the preheated oven for 25-30 minutes, or until they are tender and slightly caramelized.

4. While the vegetables are roasting, cook the lentils according to package instructions. Drain any excess liquid and set aside.

5. Once the vegetables are d2, assemble the bowls by dividing the roasted vegetables and lentils among four bowls. Top each bowl with avocado slices, crumbled feta cheese (if using), and fresh cilantro (if using).

6. Serve immediately.

Chicken With Shiitake Mushroom Vinaigrette

Ingredients:

- 6 tbsp coconut oil, melted

- 1 tsp whole grain mustard

- 3 tbsp balsamic vinegar

- 4 tbsp finely chopped flat-leaf parsley, and some for garnish

- 5 large shiitake mushrooms, remove stems

- 4 b2-in, skin-on chicken breasts

- 3 tbsp extra-virgin olive oil

- Salt and black pepper to taste

Directions:

1. Turn the grill set to high.

2. Brush all sides of the mushroom caps with coconut oil then season with salt and pepper.

3. Add the mushrooms, cap-side down, to a tray then place in the grill and cook for about 4–5 minutes. The mushrooms should only be slightly charred. Flip them over and cook for another 3–4 minutes.

4. Remove the mushrooms from the grill and chop coarsely.

5. In a medium bowl, whisk the parsley, olive oil, mustard, and vinegar, then season with salt and pepper. Add this mixture to the mushrooms and stir until fully coated.

6. Let this mixture rest at room temperature for 15 minutes before serving.

7. Brush the remaining coconut oil on both sides of the chicken and sprinkle it with salt and pepper.

8. With the grill still set on high, add the chicken, skin-side down, and cook until golden brown,

roughly 4–5 minutes. Lower the heat to medium and flip the chicken to cook on the other side for 7 minutes.

9. Remove the chicken and allow it to rest for 5 minutes before serving topped with some of the shiitake vinaigrette. Garnish with the leftover parsley leaves.

Lentil Gumbo

Ingredients:

- ½ to 1 tsp Cajun mix spice

- ½ tsp cayenne

- 1 tbsp fresh thyme or 1 tsp dried

- ½ tbsp fresh oregano or ½ tsp dried

- 3 cups vegetable or chicken broth

- 2 tbsp apple cider vinegar

- ½ cup tomato sauce, salt-free

- Fresh cilantro, to garnish

- Sliced jalapeño, to garnish

- 1 can salt-free diced tomatoes, slightly drained

- 1 ½ cup chopped onion

- 2 celery ribs, chopped

- 1 cup lentils

- 1 red bell pepper, chopped

- 2 cups fresh okra, chopped

- 1 tbsp olive oil

- 1 tsp garlic, minced

- Sea salt and pepper to taste

- 1 cup cauliflower, riced (optional)

Directions:

1. Sauté the bell pepper, garlic, onion, and celery with the oil for 5 minutes in a pan until they are softened.

2. Add the spices to the mixture and cook for another minute.

3. Add the remaining vegetables, cauliflower rice (optional), broth, sauté mixture, and tomato sauce to your instant pot. Do not add salt or pepper yet.

4. Add the lid to the pressure cooker and cook at high for 12 minutes.

5. Once the pressure has been released naturally, taste the gumbo, and decide if salt or pepper is needed. Add to taste.

6. Serve the gumbo in bowls garnished with pepper flakes, cilantro, and jalapeños.

7. If you didn't add the cauliflower rice to the gumbo, you can serve the gumbo over it before serving.

Sheet Pan Butternut Squash Hash

Ingredients:

- 2 tablespoons (30 ml) avocado oil

- 2 teaspoons sea salt, plus more for seasoning

- 1 tablespoon (7 g) ground cumin

- 1 tablespoon (8 g) chili powder

- ¼ teaspoon cayenne pepper

- Black pepper to taste

- 8 large pastured eggs

- 1 butternut squash, peeled, halved, seeded, and cubed

- ½ red bell pepper, diced

- ½ green bell pepper, diced

- ½ yellow onion, diced

- Goat cheese crumbles, for garnish (optional)

Directions:

1. Preheat the oven to 425°F (220°C, or gas mark 7).

2. On a large sheet pan, combine the butternut squash, red and green bell peppers, and onion. Drizzle the vegetables with the oil and season with the salt, cumin, chili powder, cayenne, and black pepper to taste. Use your hands to toss the veggies, evenly coating them in the oil and seasonings.

3. Bake the hash for 30 minutes. Remove from the oven. Use a spatula to divide the hash into 8 equal mounds, and make an indentation in the center of each. Crack 1 egg into the center of each mound. Season with more salt and pepper to taste.

4. Return the sheet pan to the oven and bake for 10 to 15 minutes more, depending on your desired d2ness for the eggs.

5. Sprinkle the hash with goat cheese (if using) to serve.

Avocado Latke "Toast"

Ingredients:

Yam latkes

- ¼ cup plus 2 tablespoons ground flaxseed

- ½ teaspoon garlic powder

- ½ teaspoon black pepper

- ¼ cup avocado oil

- 3 pasture-raised egg whites, beaten

- 3 cups grated Japanese white yam (or any type of yam/sweet potato)

- ¾ cup grated white onion

- 1 small jalapeño, seeds and ribs removed, finely chopped (optional)

Fennel slaw

- 2 tablespoons fresh lemon juice

- 1 tablespoon extra virgin olive oil

- 1/8 teaspoon sea salt

- ¼ teaspoon black pepper

- 1 large fennel bulb with fronds

- 10 fresh mint leaves, torn

- 2 tablespoons sundried tomatoes, chopped

- 1 small shallot, finely chopped

Smashed avocado

- 1 large avocado, halved and pitted

- ½ cup fresh cilantro, tightly packed

- Juice and zest of 1 lime

- 1 small jalapeño, seeds and ribs removed,
  finely chopped (optional)

- 1 tablespoon extra virgin olive oil

- ¼ teaspoon black pepper

Soft-boiled eggs

- 4 pasture-raised eggs

Directions:

1. Preheat the oven to 375°F and line a baking sheet with parchment paper.

2. For the latkes: Add the grated yams and onion to a fine strainer and press to remove excess moisture. In a large bowl, mix the jalapeño (if using), ground flaxseed, garlic powder, pepper, avocado oil, and egg whites together.

3. Add the yams and onions and mix well until combined.

4. Pack the mixture into a ¼-cup measuring cup and turn out each latke onto the sheet. Use your hands to flatten. You should have 8 latkes minimum.

5. Bake for 15 minutes, flip, and bake for another 15 minutes until golden brown and crispy.

6. Prepare the salad by removing the stalks and fronds from the fennel bulb. Coarsely chop the fronds and thinly slice the stalks.

7. Place in a large bowl. Using a mandolin, thinly slice the bulb, cutting it in half if necessary.

8. Add the fennel to the bowl along with the torn mint and chopped sundried tomatoes.

9. In a separate small bowl, add the minced shallots, lemon juice, olive oil, salt, and pepper.

10. Prepare the smashed avocado by scooping the avocado into a small bowl and roughly mashing it.

11. Add the cilantro, lime juice, lime zest, jalapeño (if using), olive oil, and pepper. Mix until combined but chunky.

12. To make the soft-boiled eggs, bring a large
    saucepan of water to a boil over medium-high
    heat. Using a slotted spoon, carefully lower
    the eggs into the water 2 at a time.

13. Cook for exactly 6½ minutes, adjusting the
    heat to maintain a gentle boil. Transfer the
    eggs to a bowl of ice water and chill for 2
    minutes.

14. Once cooled, gently crack the eggs and peel.

15. Combine the fennel mixture with the dressing.
    Assemble the dish by layering 2 yam latke
    with smashed avocado, adding another latke,
    then a scoop of salad, and topping with an
    egg. Repeat to make 4 total and serve.

Coconut Sesame Rice Noodles & Leek Casserole

Ingredients:

- 1/3 cup mirepoix

- 1 cup potatoes, cubed

- 1 cup edamame

- 1 cup asparagus spears

- 1 can organic crushed or stewed tomatoes

- 1 ¼ cup + 1 tablespoon beef or veggie stock
  (water works too)

- 1 teaspoon sesame oil

- 1 ½ tablespoon coconut oil

- 2 leeks, washed and sliced

- ½ teaspoon garlic, minced

- ½ cup worth rice noodles, uncooked

Directions:

1. In Dutch oven add coconut oil, sliced leeks, minced garlic, mirepoix and sauté 2-3 minutes. Add in cubed potatoes, edamame, asparagus spears, tomatoes, stock or water, uncooked rice noodles. Stir well.

2. Bring to a boil, cover, reduce heat, let simmer 20-25

Rosemary Watermelon & Cucumber Salad

Ingredients:

- 1 cup olive oil

- ½ teaspoon of red or white wine vinegar

- ½ tablespoon rosemary, diced

- ½ tablespoon Italian oregano, diced

- ½ tablespoon parsley, diced

- 1 can of garbanzo beans drained and washed (chickpeas)

- 4 cups chunked watermelon

- 1 seedless cucumber, sliced

- 2 diced scallions

Directions:

1. Mix together olive oil, wine vinegar, diced rosemary, diced oregano, diced parsley, diced scallions. Cover and chill.
2. In a large bowl mix together drained and washed garbanzo beans, watermelon chunks, cucumber slices.
3. Pour vinaigrette over salad, toss, serve!

Classic Blackened Chicken

Ingredients:

- ¼ teaspoon cayenne pepper

- ¼ teaspoon ground cumin

- ¼ teaspoon dried thyme

- 1/8 teaspoon ground white pepper

- 1/8 teaspoon onion powder

- ½ teaspoon paprika

- 1/8 teaspoon salt

- 2 chicken breasts, b2less and skinless

Directions:

1. Preheat your oven to 350 degrees Fahrenheit

2. Grease baking sheet

3. Take a cast-iron skillet and place it over high heat

4. Add oil and heat it up for 5 minutes until smoking hot

5. Take a small bowl and mix salt, paprika, cumin, white pepper, cayenne, thyme, onion powder

6. Oil the chicken breast on both sides and coat the breast with the spice mix

7. Transfer to your hot pan and cook for 1 minute per side

8. Transfer to your prepared baking sheet and bake for 5 minutes

9. Serve and enjoy!

Stir-Fried Chicken Meal

Ingredients:

- 3 stalks celery, chopped

- 1 and ½ teaspoons garlic, minced

- 1 cup chicken broth

- 2 tablespoons coconut aminos

- 1 tablespoon ginger, minced

- 1 teaspoon arrowroot

- ½ cup onions, sliced

- 2 tablespoons sesame garlic-flavoured oil

- 4 cups Bok-Choy, shredded

- 4 b2less chicken breast, cooked and sliced

Directions:

1. Add bok choy, celery in a skillet alongside 1 tablespoon of garlic oil

2. Stir fry until the bok choy is tender

3. Add the rest of the Ingredients:except arrowroot

4. If the mixture is too thin, pour a mixture of ½ a cup of cold water and arrowroot into the skillet

5. Bring the whole mixture to a 1-minute boil

6. Remove the heat source

7. Stir in coconut aminos and let it sit for 4 minutes until thick Serve and enjoy!

Hot Pink Beet Smoothie

Ingredients:

- 1 medium beet, peeled, chopped

- 2 tablespoons chia seeds

- 1/8 teaspoon sea salt

- ½ teaspoon vanilla extract, unsweetened

- 4 tablespoons almond butter

- 2 cups almond milk, unsweetened

- 2 Clementine, peeled

- 1 cup raspberries

- 1 banana, peeled

Directions:

1. In the container of a high-speed food processor or blender, combine all of the Ingredients: in the order specified in the Ingredients: list and then cover with the lid.

2. Pulse for 1 minute until smooth, and then serve.

Pumpkin Spice Oatmeal

Ingredients:

- ½ teaspoon pumpkin pie spice

- ½ teaspoon vanilla extract, unsweetened

- 1/3 cup pumpkin puree

- 2 tablespoons chopped pecans

- ¼ cup Medjool dates, pitted, chopped

- 2/3 cup rolled oats

- 1 tablespoon maple syrup

- 1 cup almond milk, unsweetened

Directions:

1. Take a medium pot, place it over medium heat, and then add all the Ingredients: except for pecans and maple syrup.

2. Stir all the Ingredients: until combined, and then cook for 5 minutes until the oatmeal has absorbed all the liquid and thickened to the desired level.

3. When d2, divide oatmeal evenly between 3 bowls, top with pecans, drizzle with maple syrup and then serve.